VEHICLES ON THE JOB

SPACE VEHICLES

BY JAMES BOW

Norwood House Press

Cover: The *New Horizons* spacecraft took many photos of Pluto.

Norwood House Press
P.O. Box 316598
Chicago, Illinois 60631

For information regarding Norwood House Press, please visit our website at: www.norwoodhousepress.com or call 866-565-2900.

PHOTO CREDITS: Cover: © Johns Hopkins University Applied Physics Laboratory/Southwest Research Institute/NASA; © Bill Ingalls/NASA, 7; © Harrison H. Schmitt/NASA, 10–11; © JPL/NASA, 12; © Ken Thornsley/NASA, 14–15; © NASA, 16, 18–19, 21; © NASA/Science Source, 9; © RGB Ventures/SuperStock/Alamy, 4–5

© 2019 by Norwood House Press.

All rights reserved.

No part of this book may be reproduced without written permission from the publisher.

LIBRARY OF CONGRESS CATALOGING-IN-PUBLICATION DATA

Names: Bow, James, author.
Title: Space vehicles / by James Bow.
Description: Chicago, Illinois : Norwood House Press, [2018] | Series: Vehicles on the job | Includes bibliographical references and index.
Identifiers: LCCN 2018003249 (print) | LCCN 2018011786 (ebook) | ISBN 9781684042258 (ebook) | ISBN 9781599539416 (hardcover : alk. paper)
Subjects: LCSH: Space vehicles--Juvenile literature.
Classification: LCC TL795 (ebook) | LCC TL795 .B69 2018 (print) | DDC 629.4--dc23
LC record available at https://lccn.loc.gov/2018003249

312N—072018
Manufactured in the United States of America in North Mankato, Minnesota.

CONTENTS

CHAPTER 1
Preparing to Launch.................................. 5

CHAPTER 2
Rockets to Space....................................... 8

CHAPTER 3
Rovers on Other Worlds 11

CHAPTER 4
Long-Range Probes................................. 15

CHAPTER 5
Future Space Vehicles 19

GLOSSARY 22
FOR MORE INFORMATION 23
INDEX 24
ABOUT THE AUTHOR............................... 24

Note: Words that are **bolded** in the text are defined in the glossary.

Crawler-transporters have moved rockets to the launch pad for more than 50 years!

CHAPTER 1

PREPARING TO LAUNCH

Huge doors open on one of the largest buildings in the world. At **NASA**'s Kennedy Space Center in Florida, the air rumbles. A rocket moves into the open.

The rocket stands on a huge moveable platform. The platform sits on a giant vehicle. The vehicle weighs over six million pounds (2.7 million kg). But it can carry twice that. It is over 130 feet (40 m) long and 114 feet (35 m) wide. It is the size of a baseball infield!

This vehicle is a crawler-transporter. It is so huge there are two drivers! They sit in separate **cabs**. The drivers move the vehicle to the launch pad several miles away.

Rockets are some of the fastest vehicles. But they start their journey on a vehicle that only goes 1 mile (1.6 km) in an hour! Crawler-transporters have moved rockets to the launch pad since 1967. They helped the Apollo 11 spacecraft get to the Moon. They carried many **space shuttles**. Now, they're taking new rockets toward the stars.

CHAPTER 2

ROCKETS TO SPACE

To get into space, we need to beat Earth's gravity. To do that, objects need to travel 4.7 miles (7.6 km) per second. This is called **orbital velocity**.

Rockets are one of the few things that can go that fast. Some rockets fire in stages. The rocket is made of several segments called stages.

Each stage has an engine and fuel. The first stage ignites its fuel and blasts off. When the fuel runs out, the rocket lets go of that stage. Then, another stage fires. Once a spacecraft reaches orbital velocity, it enters **orbit** around the Earth.

Dropping each stage makes the rocket lighter. This helps it use less fuel.

NASA's space shuttle program ran from 1981 to 2011. Rockets blasted shuttles into space! Their huge external fuel tanks could only be used once. But space shuttles were reusable. They could blast out of orbit and glide back to Earth on their wings.

The Saturn V was the biggest rocket NASA ever made. It weighed 6.54 million pounds (2.97 million kg). Scientists are looking at other ways to get into space. But for now, rockets remain the easiest way to get us there.

Astronauts left the LRVs on the Moon, so they're still there today!

ROVERS ON OTHER WORLDS

Have you ever wanted to drive on another world? In the 1970s, astronauts actually did! They drove Lunar Roving Vehicles (LRVs) on the Moon. These "moon buggies" had seats, wheels, and a controller for steering. They were open on top, without doors, windows, or a roof. They ran on battery power.

The other vehicles that have driven on other worlds are robots. The first was *Sojourner*. It weighed just 23 pounds (10.5 kg). It was **solar** powered. It had three cameras as well as instruments to analyze rocks. It proved scientists could land a vehicle on Mars and control it from Earth.

Other robots followed. *Spirit* and *Opportunity* were bigger vehicles. They weighed 408 pounds (185 kg).

Sojourner's mission was only supposed to last for 7 days, but it lasted 83!

Their wheels could move over rocks or soft sand. They were also powered by the sun.

These robots each had an arm with a tool to study rocks. The arms had other equipment to photograph and study the soil. The rovers looked for signs of water on Mars. Later, the *Phoenix* lander found ice on the planet.

The rover *Curiosity* arrived on Mars in 2012 with even more equipment. It weighed nearly 1 ton (0.9 metric tons).

In total, the four rovers sent to Mars have now traveled many miles. *Sojourner* and *Spirit* have stopped working. *Opportunity* and *Curiosity* were still sending data back to Earth in 2018. They will be joined by a new rover in 2021.

A rocket launched the *New Horizons* probe into space in 2006. It didn't reach Pluto until 2015!

CHAPTER 4

LONG-RANGE PROBES

Our **solar system** is huge! Even our fastest rockets take months just to get to Mars. And Mars is Earth's neighbor! Fortunately, robots can go where humans can't.

Robot probes travel vast distances through space. They often have metal frames with large antennae. The antennae allow them to send data back to Earth.

Many carry powerful telescopes. Some get power from the sun.

Robot probes have visited every planet in our solar system. Some probes have gone very far. *Voyager 2* took spectacular pictures of Jupiter, Saturn, Uranus, and Neptune. *Voyager 1* is now over 13 billion miles (21 billion km) from the Sun. More recently, *New Horizons* passed by Pluto. It is going to explore the **Kuiper Belt**.

Voyager 1 and *Voyager 2* have been traveling for more than 40 years!

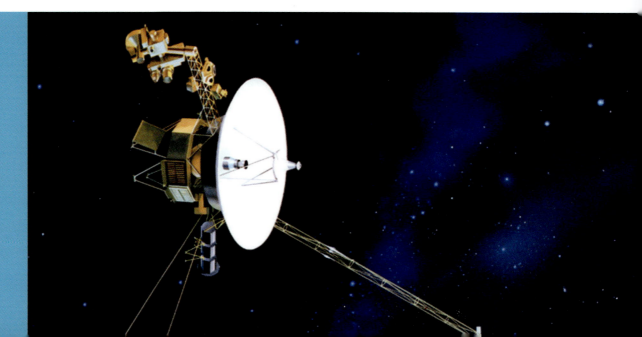

STEM AT WORK: POWER IN SPACE

Scientists face all kinds of challenges when deciding how to power a spacecraft. Space is a harsh place to be. If something goes wrong, no one can head off across the solar system to fix a broken ship. And, there must be power to keep a mission going for many, many years.

Scientists are working on new solutions to these problems. They know solar power works well for spacecraft that are close to the sun. Probes that head out across the solar system need something different. Scientists are working on solar panels that work farther from the sun. Special batteries are being developed, too. And, scientists are finding ways to use other forms of energy more efficiently.

NASA also sent the *Dawn* probe to the asteroid belt. In the future, robots could be sent to mine asteroids and bring the material back to Earth.

The Orion spacecraft will allow humans to travel farther into space than ever before.

CHAPTER 5

FUTURE SPACE VEHICLES

There is much to explore in our solar system. People are planning to send astronauts to the Moon and Mars. The search for life on other planets may send probes to the moons of Jupiter and Saturn.

ON THE JOB: ROCKET SCIENTISTS

Do you want to become a rocket scientist? Study math and physics at school. Build things with LEGO bricks. Look for junior engineer events. In college, study **aerospace engineering**.

Teams of scientists send rockets into space. Scientists imagine, design, build, and test rockets and spacecraft. They study data sent back from space. Then they dream up and plan for the next missions to space!

NASA is designing the Orion spacecraft. It could send people to Mars. This mission will take many years. The Orion spacecraft can carry four people. It holds enough food, water, and oxygen for the mission.

Others want to open up space to more people. SpaceX is working on reusable rockets. These will make space travel less expensive. Virgin Galactic is planning to build spaceships that could fly tourists into space.

Would you like to go out into space yourself? Would you like to visit the Moon or Mars? Soon, maybe you can!

SpaceX is designing new rockets. The company wants to send people to Mars.

GLOSSARY

aerospace engineering (EHR-oh-spase en-juh-NIHR-ing): The designing and building of airplanes and spacecraft.

cabs (CABS): Covered areas where the operator of a truck or other machine can sit or stand.

Kuiper Belt (KEYE-puhr BELT): An area of the solar system beyond Neptune that is full of comets, asteroids, and dwarf planets.

NASA (NAH-suh): The National Aeronautics and Space Administration. A US government organization in charge of space-related science and technology.

orbit (OR-biht): The path something takes when it circles around something.

orbital velocity (OR-bih-tull veh-LAH-suh-tee): The speed needed to reach orbit.

solar (SO-luhr): Relating to the sun.

solar system (SO-luhr SIHS-tuhm): A sun and the planets that orbit around it.

space shuttles (SPASE SHUT-ulls): Vehicles that NASA used for space missions until 2011.

FOR MORE INFORMATION

BOOKS

Loomis, Evan, and Levi Bethune. *Elon Musk: This Book Is About Rockets*. Herndon, VA: Mascot Books, 2017. Discover how Elon Musk founded SpaceX and how he plans to change the future of rockets.

Wallace, Karen. *Rockets and Spaceships*. New York, NY: DK Publishing, 2011. Find out how rockets and spaceships take people into space.

Zobel, Derek. *NASA*. Minneapolis, MN: Bellwether Media, 2010. Meet the people at NASA who create and build rockets.

WEBSITES

Discovery Kids – Space
www.discoverymindblown.com/category/space
Learn about our solar system with interactive games and videos.

NASA Kids' Club
www.nasa.gov/kidsclub/index.html
Learn all about space and space exploration through games, videos, and articles.

INDEX

A
Apollo 11, 6

C
crawler-transporter, 5, 6

L
launch pad, 6
Lunar Roving Vehicle (LRV), 11, 12

M
Mars, 12, 13, 15, 19, 20, 21
Mars rover, 11, 12, 13
Moon, 6, 11, 19, 21

N
NASA, 5, 9, 17, 20

P
probe, 15–17, 19

R
rocket, 5, 6, 8, 9, 15, 20

S
solar power, 12, 13, 16, 17
solar system, 15, 16, 17, 19
space shuttle, 6, 9

ABOUT THE AUTHOR

James Bow is the author of more than 40 educational books for children and young adults, a novelist, and a local columnist. He graduated from the University of Waterloo School of Urban and Regional Planning in 1991. Born in Toronto, he now lives in Kitchener, Ontario, Canada, with his author wife and his two daughters.